CONFLICT
IN
SOMALIA AND ETHIOPIA

Patrick Gilkes

Wayland

Conflicts

Titles in the series:
Conflict in Eastern Europe
Conflict in the Middle East
Conflict in Somalia and Ethiopia
Conflict in Southern Africa
The Breakup of the Soviet Union
The Breakup of Yugoslavia

Cover: Armed Eritrean villagers in 1985. The struggle for independence in Eritrea was of major political and military significance to Ethiopia throughout the 1980s.

Title page: Somali gunmen of the USC in an armoured 'technical' vehicle in Baidoa, September 1992.

Picture acknowledgements
The publishers would like to thank the following for supplying their photographs for use as illustrations in this book: Camera Press 11, 12 (Sarah Errington), 14 (Marion Kaplan), 15 (Marion Kaplan), 17 (Mike Wells), 19 (Istvan Bara), 20 (Tudor Lomas), 21 (El Koussy), 27 (Fiona McDougall), 28 (Norman Sagansky), 32 (Gavin Smith), 34, 36 (Marion Kaplan), 37 (Marion Kaplan), 42, 43, 45 below (J. Melandez); Robert Estall cover (Angela Fisher and Carol Beckwith), 13 (Angela Fisher and Carol Beckwith), 24 (David Coulson), 40 (David Coulson); Image Select 7 (Archiv fur Kunst und Geschichte, Berlin); Impact Photos 29 (Peter Menzel), 31 (Peter Menzel); Link Picture Library title page (Zed Nelson); Christine Osborne Pictures 5, 9, 16; Topham Picture Library 10 (Press Association), 22 (Associated Press), 23 (Associated Press), 33 (Associated Press), 35 (Associated Press/ Hassan Amini), 38 (Associated Press), 45 top (Associated Press).
The maps on pages 4, 8, 17, 26, and 30 were supplied by Peter Bull.

Series editor: William Wharfe
Editor: Judy Martin
Designer/Typesetter: Malcolm Walker/Kudos Editorial and Design Services

First published in 1994 by
Wayland (Publishers) Ltd
61 Western Road, Hove
East Sussex BN3 1JD

© Copyright 1994 Wayland (Publishers) Limited

British Library Cataloguing in Publication Data
Gilkes, Patrick
  Conflict in Somalia and Ethiopia. – (Conflicts Series)
  I. Title II. Series
  967.7305

ISBN 0-7502-1179-2

Printed and bound in Italy by G. Canale & C.S.p.A., Turin

Contents

CHAPTER 1

INTRODUCTION

Somalia and Ethiopia are the two main countries in the Horn of Africa, an area that has been in acute crisis since 1974 and has a long history of conflict. Ethiopia is an old-established African state, formerly a powerful empire. Somalia came into existence as a unified state only in 1960, combining territories that were previously colonies of Britain and Italy. But the Somali people have traditionally occupied several regions of the Horn, and many still live outside the boundaries of the Somali state.

Conflict within Ethiopia from the 1960s to the 1990s was often dominated by the struggle of Eritrea, the northern region, to obtain independence. Eritrea broke free in 1991, at the same time as liberation fighters replaced the central government of Ethiopia with a new regime; it formally became an independent state in May 1993. The northern part of Somalia declared itself independent in May 1991, as the Republic of Somaliland. There have been other liberation movements in Ethiopia, and control in southern Somalia was split between factions throughout the early 1990s.

The problem of unity led the armed forces in both Somalia and Ethiopia to take power during the 1970s. Ethiopia was a multinational state, and it was feared that if the rebels fighting for independence in Eritrea succeeded, then other

Countries of the Horn of Africa today, including the new state of Eritrea and the still unrecognized state of Somaliland. Notice how narrow the bottom of the Red Sea is at the Bab el Mandeb straits, giving countries in this region the potential to control an important shipping route.

Ethiopia has suffered often from drought and famine, but when the rains do come, the highlands are green and fertile.

regions or peoples within Ethiopia would try to do the same. The Ethiopian army felt not enough was being done to keep the country united. In Somalia, the military overthrew the civilian government in 1969 in order to work more actively to take over Somali-inhabited areas outside Somalia itself.

Marxism and superpower rivalry

To carry out their aims, the military leaders Colonel Mengistu in Ethiopia and General Siad Barre in Somalia chose to use Marxist policies. In both cases, this was a surprising choice. The ruling groups in Ethiopia were Christian; the Somalis were Muslims. Both religions regarded Marxism as 'godless'. Neither Mengistu nor Siad Barre really believed that Marxism would change people's lives, but it provided a method for setting up a highly organized party structure able to gain and keep tight control of government and all aspects of society.

Marxism helped them to gain alliance with one of the major superpowers, the Soviet Union, which between 1960 and 1988 was prepared to be generous to regimes which claimed to be socialist or Marxist. Both the Soviet Union and its rival superpower, the USA, were interested in the strategic position of the Horn of Africa. It is situated where the Red Sea meets the Indian Ocean, close to the Persian Gulf and the oilfields there and in Saudi Arabia. Access to oil resources was important to the superpowers.

During the period of 'Cold War' after the Second World War, when relations between the USA and Soviet Union were hostile, they sought allies in other countries throughout the world. Governments or political organizations favoured by one superpower would be unlikely to get help from the other, but if an alliance with one broke down, the other might step in. The rivalry continued to a lesser extent through the 1980s and ceased altogether with the collapse of the Soviet Union in 1991.

As well as military conflicts, the Horn of Africa has suffered devastating effects from large-scale famines. Governments and guerrilla factions in Ethiopia and Somalia have been dependent on foreign aid for supplies of weapons and food. Both countries showed great skill in manipulating the superpowers – Ethiopia, for example, got weapons from the Soviet Union and food aid from the USA through most of the 1980s. But from the mid-1980s, the USA made it clear that it would only support organizations committed to multi-party democracy, and some abandoned Marxism for that reason.

COLONIZATION AND RESISTANCE

Serious European interest in Africa began with the Portuguese in the sixteenth century. Before 1800, contacts were largely commercial and based on the slave trade. There was little European settlement, except by the Dutch in South Africa. Relations between African powers and European states were founded on a basis of equality. For example, the Portuguese made treaties with the Kings of Kongo (now northern Angola), whom they converted to Christianity, and with the Emperors of Monomotapa (now Zimbabwe).

The slave trade played the main role in altering the power balance in Africa. Areas became depopulated, particularly near the coasts, as their people were taken into slavery. Alliances made with the slave traders led to fighting between neighbouring African states, which raided each other for people and goods.

During the nineteenth century, Europe went through an industrial revolution which provided greatly improved weaponry. This coincided with European exploration of Africa, where explorers found a continent that had been devastated in parts by the slave trade. Europeans made the assumption that their own civilization was superior, and that they should pursue a Christian missionary role to 'civilize' Africa, by force if necessary.

Another important element was the rivalry of European powers, which extended to colonization of the newly explored territories. At the Berlin Conference of 1884, the main imperial powers – Britain, France, Germany, Italy and Belgium – agreed to recognize each other's 'spheres of influence' in Africa.

European take-over was strongly resisted by the dozens of African states and chiefdoms. Leaders like Samori Toure (died 1900) in West Africa or the Mahdi (1844-85) in Sudan fought successfully for years against European imperialism. The colonizing powers suffered many defeats, but their superior weaponry and fire-power proved too great for the African resistance. By 1914 almost all of Africa was under colonial rule, with two exceptions. One was the state of Liberia, founded by freed American slaves in 1820 and made independent in 1847. The other was Ethiopia.

THE LEGEND OF PRESTER JOHN

During the Christian-Muslim wars over Jerusalem in the thirteenth and fourteenth centuries (called the Crusades in Western Europe), the Christian armies heard tales of a mysterious empire 'beyond Islam', variously thought to be in China, central Asia or deepest Africa. Its ruler was Prester John, a Christian priest and king who ruled over ninety-nine other kings. Some said he was the guardian of the Holy Grail, a magical dish used by Jesus Christ at the Last Supper. The Crusaders expected that Prester John would come to their aid.

The origin of the story appears to have been the Ethiopian empire, whose Christian emperor had the title Negusse Negest – King of Kings.

Menelik II, Emperor of Ethiopia 1889-1913, responsible for expanding Ethiopia to its present extent. He was named after the mythical first emperor of Ethiopia, Menelik I, who was supposed to be the son of King Solomon and the Queen of Sheba. All Ethiopian emperors claimed descent from Solomon.

The Ethiopian empire

Ethiopia, like Egypt, had a long history as a unified state, although its size and strength varied at different times. Between about 1780 and 1850, imperial authority had virtually collapsed, and several kingdoms and leaders fought for power. In the later nineteenth century a series of strong rulers reimposed authority and expanded the empire. Yohannis IV (ruled 1872-89) defeated invasions by the Egyptians, Italians and the Mahdists of Sudan. Menelik II (ruled 1889-1914) defeated a 20,000-strong Italian army at the battle of Adua in 1889.

Ethiopia recovered its strength at just the right time and was fortunate in being targeted by the weakest of the European powers. Italy later took revenge when it overran Ethiopia in 1936, but in 1896 it had to accept defeat. Despite his success, however, Menelik was having trouble controlling his army, and to avoid further conflict he allowed the Italians to keep the northern region of Eritrea. He regarded this as a short-term solution – for Ethiopians, Eritrea remained a part of the motherland that would one day return. But giving up Eritrea helped Menelik to reach agreements with Britain and France, countries friendly toward Italy, over fixing his boundaries in other parts of Ethiopia.

Somalis divided

During the 1880s and 1890s, the Ethiopian empire expanded rapidly to the west, south and east.

Ethiopia had traditional claims to some of these areas, but other parts had never been under Ethiopian rule before. This expansion, and that of European colonialism, affected the nomadic Somali people who lived in the easternmost regions of the Horn of Africa, from the Tana river in Kenya to Djibouti on the northern coast.

British interest in territories occupied by Somalis was originally to prevent the French from expanding out of their colony in Djibouti. The British, who also wanted meat supplies for their own colony at Aden on the other side of the Red Sea, signed a series of treaties with Somali clan leaders and declared a protectorate over their northern areas in 1886. The Italians did the same in the south. There was resistance, most notably from Mohammed Abdullah Hussein, the Sayeed, a religious leader famous for his poetry as well as his military skills. He fought for twenty years against the British, Italians and Ethiopians, combining the religious fervour of Islam with a call for Somali nationalism. Not all Somali clans followed him, but it was not until his death in 1920 that all three powers were able to establish full control in the Horn of Africa.

By 1900, the Somalis were divided between five different territories: Djibouti, then called the French Territory of the Afars and Issas; British Somaliland; Italian Somaliland; the Ogaden region of Ethiopia; and the British colony of Kenya, bordering Ethiopia to the south. Colonial boundaries cut across clan lands, and three of the major clan families were seriously divided. Throughout the colonial history of the region, there were many cross-border raids caused by the territorial divisions.

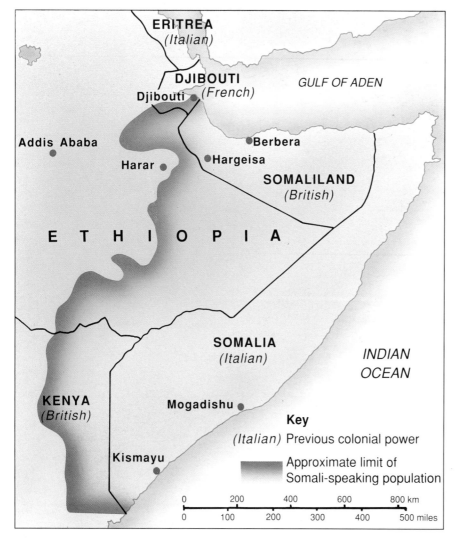

The division of Somali lands by colonial powers, showing what shares the British, Ethiopians, French, and Italians took. Modern state boundaries represent areas formerly occupied by European colonial powers. There was no state of Somalia at any time before 1960, but all Somalis spoke the same language and thought of themselves as the same people.

Somali nomads loading up camels to leave the railside town of Dire Dawa in north-eastern Ethiopia.

Colonial rule

Colonialism in Africa varied enormously. The Germans were efficient but brutal, violently subduing any local resistance. The Italians attempted to rule by force but encountered greater conflict, as in Libya, where ten years of fighting ended with the Italians forced to sign a treaty out of weakness rather than strength. The French governed their colonies as part of a 'greater France', as if they were regions of the home country. Britain ruled each of its colonies separately, often governing through the traditional African rulers, and allowed them to assume that they would gain independence.

In every case, economic and social developments among African societies were disrupted. Agricultural and industrial production were organized for the benefit of the colonial power; mineral wealth and raw materials were taken out of the colonies for processing, and finished goods were sold back in. Control was exercised from European capitals where politicians had little knowledge of African culture, and less interest.

In 1960, the independent Republic of Somalia was created from British Somaliland and Italian Somaliland. To ensure unity, the new Somali state encouraged the idea that the Somali-speaking areas in Djibouti, Kenya and Ethiopia should join the republic. The aim was symbolized by the five-pointed star on the Somali flag, each point representing a traditional Somali area.

Somali efforts to unite the scattered territories form one continuous thread through recent conflicts in the Horn of Africa. Almost immediately after independence, liberation fronts were set up. The activity of the Western Somalia Liberation Front (WSLF) drew Somalia into a short border war with Ethiopia in 1963. The Front for the Liberation of the Somali Coast, in Djibouti, and the Northern Frontier District Liberation Front, in Kenya, achieved little.

SETTING THE SCENE FOR CONFLICT

Ethiopia's last emperor was Haile Selassie, born in 1892, made Crown Prince and Regent in 1916, crowned Emperor in 1930, and deposed in 1974. He came to power when Ethiopia was a largely feudal society, with great lords exercising almost total authority in their own regions. He left it with the basis for a centralized, if only partly modernized state, with a constitution, a standing army, and Amharic as a national language. He also abolished slavery within Ethiopia, in 1926.

The process of change was interrupted by the Italian invasion of 1935. Italy tried to justify this action by claiming that Ethiopia's borders with neighbouring colonies had not been satisfactorily agreed during Menelik's time. Italian forces took the Ethiopian capital, Addis Ababa, in May 1936 and Haile Selassie fled to Europe to make an unsuccessful appeal to the League of Nations. He then went to live in Bath, in the west of England.

Haile Selassie, the last Emperor of Ethiopia, 1930-1974, seen here on a state visit to Britain in 1954. In the last decade of his rule, he took more interest in international affairs and neglected growing opposition to his autocratic, if usually benevolent rule.

Italian attempts to crush resistance led to many revolts, but it was only when Italy declared war on Britain in the Second World War that Haile Selassie got any help. Britain was concerned that Italy's forces in Ethiopia and East Africa might try to threaten Egypt, as the Italian troops in Libya did. In 1940, British forces advanced into Ethiopia from Sudan and Kenya. After a short and successful campaign, the Italians were driven out. In May 1941, Emperor Haile Selassie rode back into Addis Ababa.

With British help, Haile Selassie continued the centralization of power into his own hands. His rule was often benevolent, but it was authoritarian. His policies created an educated

Ethiopian fighters, or 'patriots', shown here attacking an Italian fort, did not have the weapons to resist the bombs and artillery of the Italian occupion forces. After Haile Selassie returned to Ethiopia in 1941, he got help from the British and then the USA to enlarge and modernize his armies.

bureaucracy and army, with which he could put down opposition, preserve his empire and secure his own position. An elected parliament was set up in 1957, but given no power. A prime minister was appointed in the 1950s, but not allowed to choose his own ministers until 1966. Labour unions were permitted in 1962, but their right to strike was very limited. A land reform bill to restrict the powers of the great landowners went before parliament in 1968, but had made no

progress by the time revolution came in 1974.

In 1960, Haile Selassie's own bodyguards had rebelled, but even this did not speed up reforms. Annual student demonstrations after 1964 highlighted corruption, the lack of jobs, and the need for land reform to give tenant farmers proper rights to their own produce. Protest also focused on the disastrous famines in Ethiopia, particularly in 1972-74, when perhaps 200,000 people died. Revolts were common, often led by members of the governing class whom Haile Selassie normally manipulated very well.

Eritreans and Somalis

Two areas of Ethiopia proved particularly difficult in the post-war period – Eritrea in the north, and the Ogaden in the south-east. The British played a particular role in both cases, as British forces had taken over the Italian colonies of Eritrea and Italian Somaliland in 1941, at the same time as helping Haile Selassie to recover his throne.

The question of who should control Eritrea after the Second World War proved complicated. Haile Selassie demanded it back as a traditional part of the Ethiopian empire. The British suggested that part of Eritrea should go to Sudan

> Haile Selassie's speech at the League of Nations in June 1936 was an impressive performance. It had little political effect at the time, but it remains a powerful appeal: '. . . If a strong Government finds that it can, with impunity, destroy a weak people, then the hour has struck for that weak people to appeal to the League of Nations to give its judgement in all freedom. God in history will remember your judgement . . . I ask the great powers, who have promised the guarantee of collective security to small states, . . . what measures do they intend to take? Representatives of the world, I have come to Geneva to discharge in your midst the most painful of the duties of the head of a state. What answer am I to take back to my people?'

(controlled by the British) and the rest should unite with the Ethiopian province of Tigrai. This would bring together the Tigrean people, who lived in both regions, in a 'Greater Tigrai'. But the events of the Second World War had brought in other interests. The Italians wanted Eritrea back; the Russians thought they could administer it; the USA had become involved when it took over the Italian radio facility in Asmara, the capital of Eritrea, in 1942. Egypt and other Muslim states were interested in Eritrea's Muslim population (about 50 per cent of the total population).

The main political groups in Eritrea itself were the Unionists, who wanted full union with Ethiopia, and the Independence Bloc, a largely Muslim organization. A four-power commission from the UK, USA, the Soviet Union and France visited Eritrea in 1949. It failed to produce a solution, but did not recommend independence. The issue was referred to the United Nations (UN), which sent its own mission. Of the five members of the mission, two finally recommended independence, two voted for federation and one for full union with Ethiopia. The UN accepted federation as a compromise. The federation came into existence in 1952 with the head of the Unionist Party as its first chief executive and a legislative body called the Eritrean Assembly.

From the beginning the relationship between Ethiopia and Eritrea was most uneasy. The British had encouraged political parties, elections, trade unions and a free press, but had done little to improve the Eritrean economy. Haile Selassie, ruler of a centralized and autocratic state, was having none of this. He regarded federation as the first step to full union. The various Eritrean institutions were gradually dismantled or incorporated into the imperial administration. Parties disappeared, the Eritrean flag was withdrawn, and in November 1962 the Eritrean Assembly voted itself out of existence and united Eritrea to the rest of Ethiopia. Some Assembly members later claimed they had been bribed, but their position had already become impossible because the Assembly had no real power.

Before the end of the federation, Eritrean nationalists began to organize opposition abroad. The Eritrean Liberation Front (ELF) was set up in 1958 in Cairo and took up armed struggle in Eritrea three years later. Seen as a largely Muslim lowland organization it did not welcome Christian Eritreans. Progress was slow and in the late 1960s it became ineffective for a time due to divisions between ELF members.

Part of Addis Ababa market. Markets vary from small village ones to the 'mercarto' area of Addis Ababa, the largest covered market in Africa. Village markets are held weekly, selling vegetables, spices, chickens and eggs, as well as household necessities such as matches, paraffin and oil.

NOMADIC PEOPLES

Much of the opposition in Ethiopia first appeared among pastoral nomadic populations in the outer areas of the state, such as the Somalis, Afars, or the Beni Amir in western Eritrea, all of whom also lived in neighbouring countries. These were groups that resisted government control: they wanted to use traditional grazing grounds at will, even where they crossed international borders, and to live their own lives without interference.

The Ethiopian governments of Emperor Haile Selassie and Colonel Mengistu, both trying to increase government control, found this unacceptable. They wanted nomadic populations to settle down, pay taxes, and stop crossing borders as they pleased. This is a common attitude among African governments; even those that claim to be democratic want to have proper control in their states. Unless governments change their attitudes to boundaries, the traditional lifestyle of nomadic peoples is unlikely to last long.

Somali nomads drawing water from a well in the Ogaden region of Ethiopia.

Unrest in the Ogaden

After the Second World War, British policy towards the Ogaden paralleled its ideas on Eritrea. Britain kept parts of the Ogaden region until 1948 and 1952, areas used for grazing by the main Somali clans in British Somaliland. The British also thought about trying to expand their control permanently, floating the idea of a 'Greater Somalia', to include British Somaliland and part or all of the Ogaden.

In the end, the Ogaden areas were given back to Ethiopia but the region remained a problem.

Its nomadic population was a target for groups seeking Somali unification after 1960. Ethiopia's attitude to the area was negative. Officials regarded postings to the Ogaden as exile, and Haile Selassie sent people there as punishment. Little was done to build services such as schools or hospitals, and where agricultural projects were started, as at Jigjiga and Gode, Christian Amhara or Tigrean settlers were brought in from the highlands. Somalis got no benefits from the improvements. When the government wanted taxes it sent out the army.

THE ETHIOPIAN REVOLUTION AND SOMALI WAR

By 1970 the weaknesses of the imperial regime in Ethiopia were clear for all to see. The threat was underlined by the fact that there had been military take-overs in Sudan and Somalia in 1969. There was widespread expectation that Ethiopia would suffer a similar change of government, though most observers thought that Haile Selassie, who would be eighty in 1972, would die in power despite the pressures of annual student disturbances, rising unemployment, inflation and the steadily rising cost of combating the guerrilla fighters in Eritrea.

It was the famines of the early 1970s that finally tipped the balance. The imperial government appeared to have ignored it. A group of military officers, the Derg, carried out a carefully organized and gradual coup. The final blow to Haile Selassie came when Ethiopian television showed a film of him eating off a gold plate and feeding steak to his dogs, while famine victims died. There was little opposition to his removal in September 1974. He stayed a prisoner in his imperial palace until his death in August 1975.

Peaceful at first, the revolution turned 'bloody' with the execution of sixty senior officials of the old regime in November 1974. Within months, various political groups were fighting to influence the Derg. It was a war fought out in the streets of Addis Ababa, in which hundreds died. Factions in the Derg took sides. Colonel Mengistu Haile Mariam took power in February 1977, executing half a dozen of his colleagues; he had his deputy shot nine months later. The army was used to intervene in conflict between left-wing groups and to put down opposition. In the 'Red Terror' of 1977-78, hundreds of people were imprisoned, tortured and killed. The struggles were supposedly about ideology; the reality was a struggle for power.

One effect of this was to allow the Eritrean guerrilla movements to make major gains. They themselves were divided, and their own divisions

Drought-stricken land in Ethiopia. In the first year of drought, stored crops can be eaten; in the second year, the seed grain; in the third, the animals, including oxen needed for ploughing; by the fourth year, if not long before, there is nothing left to eat.

MAJOR EVENTS IN ETHIOPIA, 1896-1993

1896 Italian invasion of Ethiopia defeated at battle of Adua; Italy keeps Eritrea as colony.

1908 Last of Ethiopia's boundaries with colonial powers Britain, France and Italy defined by treaty.

1930 Haile Selassie crowned emperor.

1936-41 Ethiopia occupied by Italy. Haile Selassie exiled to Britain.

1942 Haile Selassie returns; Eritrea kept by Britain.

1952 Eritrea federated to Ethiopia.

1961 Eritrean Liberation Front (ELF) launches armed struggle.

1962 Eritrea's federal status dissolved. Eritrea becomes Ethiopian province.

1968-70 Splits in ELF lead to civil war between ELF and dissident groups, which join to make up Eritrean People's Liberation Front (EPLF).

1974 Revolution in Ethiopia. Haile Selassie deposed. Declaration of Ethiopian socialism.

1977 Colonel Mengistu seizes supreme power. Red Terror campaign launched. Somali forces invade Ethiopia. Eritrean guerrillas capture all but five towns in Eritrea.

1978 Somali forces driven out. Ethiopian troops launch offensive into Eritrea.

1988 EPLF win major victory at Af Abet in northern Eritrea.

1989 Tigrai People's Liberation Front (TPLF) win major victory in Tigrai; set up Ethiopian People's Revolutionary Democratic Front (EPRDF). Attempted coup against Mengistu in May.

1990 EPLF captures Massawa and cuts off supply route of Ethiopian forces in Eritrea.

1991 Mengistu flees to Zimbabwe. EPRDF takes Addis Ababa. EPLF takes Asmara and establishes Provisional Government of Eritrea. National Conference held in Addis Ababa in July; Council of Representatives set up. EPRDF sets up new regions based on ethnicity.

1992 District and regional elections held.

1993 Addis Ababa university closed in January after students killed in demonstration against Eritrean independence. In Eritrean referendum, April, 99.8 per cent of voters in favour of independence. Eritrea formally independent in May.

University students in Addis Ababa on strike over government failure to deal with famine. The student demonstrations each year were an important element in the growing opposition to Haile Selassie every year from 1966. They did much to alert the people of Addis Ababa, and the international community, to conditions in the Ethiopian countryside.

proved irreconcilable, but even civil wars in 1972-74 and 1981-82 did not prevent progress. The two main movements, the ELF and the Eritrean People's Liberation Front (EPLF) co-operated in a major attack on the Eritrean capital, Asmara, in February 1975. Hundreds of guerrillas infiltrated the city and nearly succeeded in taking it.

It took several weeks for Ethiopian government troops to re-establish full control. Their methods and the retaliation they took, which included the massacre of several hundred people in the church of a nearby village, turned the majority of Christian Eritreans against the central government, although they had previously been in favour of incorporation into Ethiopia.

Over the next two years, with the Ethiopian army distracted by the threat from Somalia, by political divisions, and shortage of supplies for its American weapons, the ELF from the west and EPLF from the north overran most of the province. By December 1977, government forces in Eritrea were confined to the towns of Barentu, Asmara, Massawa and Adi Caieh (all under siege), and the port of Assab.

The Ogaden War, July 1977 - March 1978

Eritrean successes in the second half of 1977 came at the same time as Somali victories in the south of Ethiopia, after invasion in July. When General Mohammed Siad Barre took power in Somalia in 1969, he made a considerable effort to do away with clan politics and to emphasize Somali nationalism. An impressive literacy campaign was carried out after the choice of a script allowed Somali to become a written language. The administration and the judiciary were staffed by military personnel, to speed up activity. Prices were controlled, banks and other financial organizations were nationalized. After the adoption of socialism, a Somali Revolutionary Socialist Party was created in 1976.

The final element was the war against Ethiopia in 1977. It was a popular move, as public opinion in Somalia was behind the struggle of WSLF, the guerrilla organization of the Ogaden clan in Ethiopia. In the early stages all went well. Somali forces quickly drove through the Ogaden region, taking Jigjiga and nearly capturing Dire Dawa further north. The main city of eastern Ethiopia, Harar, was besieged. This proved to be the limit.

Colonel Mengistu, General Teferi Bante and Colonel Atnafu – the leaders of the Ethiopian revolution in 1975. Colonel Mengistu shot General Teferi when he took power himself in February 1977, and had Colonel Atnafu executed in November of the same year.

ASSAULT ON MASSAWA

The EPLF made a great effort to take the port of Massawa in December 1977. It was particularly significant as the main supply port for the Ethiopian army in Eritrea. It was also difficult to capture, as the port is on two islands connected by causeways to the mainland town. The naval base at Massawa is separate, but on a peninsula sticking out into the sea (right).

The EPLF tried to capture the naval base by assault. At 14.40 hours on 23 December 1977, nearly 3,000 guerrillas leapt over the sea wall and plunged on to the flat, open salt pans to run towards the heavily sandbagged defences. An observer said, 'It was an eerie sight. Row after row of them, bent double, sprinting in silence towards the Ethiopian defences.'

The assault was a disaster. The defenders quite literally blew the attackers away with concentrated machine-gun fire. At least half the guerrillas were killed and most of the rest were injured.

EPLF guerrillas charge across the salt pans of mainland Massawa towards the port.

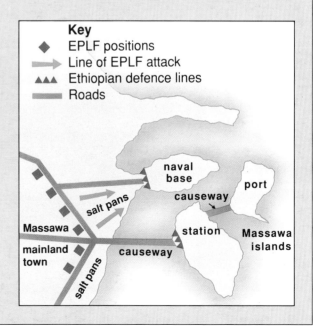

Somali forces were over-extended and running short of supplies by November, partly because the Ethiopian air force controlled the air, partly because support for Somalia from the Soviet Union had ended.

In the long run, the much larger Ethiopian army would probably have won the war, but the switch of Soviet support made the result quick and certain. When Mengistu took over Ethiopia, in February 1977, the Soviet Union decided to offer him support and warned their ally, Somalia, not to invade Ethiopia. When Siad Barre ignored their advice, they withdrew from alliance with the Somalis. The Soviet Union provided dozens of planes and hundreds of tanks to Ethiopia, and arranged for nearly 20,000 troops from their close ally, Cuba, to help drive the Somalis out in Ethiopia's counteroffensive of February 1978.

Three weeks later, the war was over. The cost was enormous. Casualties ran into tens of thousands and neither side had taken prisoners. Hundreds of thousands of refugees from the Ogaden fled into Somalia, fearing Ethiopian reprisals. The Somali army was left divided and bitter. The lack of help for demobilized soldiers, the loss of military equipment, and the executions of some officers accused of not fighting well all caused unrest and uncertainty.

There was an attempted coup in April 1978. Siad Barre had no difficulty in crushing the revolt, but the legacy of the war was a steady erosion of his own position and power. He was blamed for the loss of the Soviet alliance, which led to a shortage of weapons, and for his failure to replace it with an alliance with the USA. The costs of the refugees crippled the country's already poor economy, despite help from international aid agencies, and left the Somali government with fewer resources than before.

The Gode bridge, destroyed by retreating Somali troops in March 1978. It was the only bridge over the Webi Shebelli river. The war caused massive destruction in the Ogaden, but the worst damage came as Somali troops retreated, blowing up the bridge as well as irrigation works for agricultural settlements at Gode and ploughing up the airfield.

THE ERITREAN WAR

The Ethiopian army, flushed with its success against Somalia and backed up by enormous supplies of Soviet-made equipment, turned back to Eritrea. Even before the Somali invasion the government had started to organize a 300,000-strong 'people's militia' to fight in Eritrea. In 1978, 100,000 fresh troops were deployed along the border. The ELF and the EPLF, over-confident of their strength, abandoned their previously successful guerrilla tactics to face the government forces on a conventional basis, using captured tanks and artillery. But the two organizations kept their forces separate and failed to reunite even in the face of military threat. Government forces, careless of casualties, and with infinitely greater firepower, quickly retook nearly all the towns they had lost.

By the end of the year, the ELF had suffered heavy losses and was forced to return to guerrilla operations. The EPLF withdrew to the far north-west of Eritrea, around the remote town of Nacfa. There the Ethiopian army lost momentum, and failed to capture the town in a series of unsuccessful offensives from 1979 to 1987. The war degenerated into a stalemate, with the EPLF digging hundreds of kilometres of trenches in the arid mountains of northern Eritrea where the Ethiopian army could not deploy its heavy artillery and tanks.

One effect of the Ethiopian victories was another outbreak of fighting between the ELF and the EPLF. In 1982, after a year of civil war, the EPLF drove ELF forces out of Eritrea and into Sudan. There they were largely disarmed by the Sudanese, and the movement broken into several factions. As a result, the ELF played little direct part in the subsequent fighting, while the EPLF's victories left it as the only real force in the struggle for Eritrean independence.

An Eritrean fighter in the trenches around Nacfa. Women played a major role in the Eritrean movements, particularly the EPLF. A third of the EPLF fighters were female and a major effect was to raise the status of women in Eritrean society, though Eritrea, like Ethiopia and Somalia, remains male-dominated.

However, various ELF groups retained considerable support through the 1980s and 1990s, particularly among the Muslims in western Eritrea and the many thousands of refugees who fled to Sudan during the war years.

In 1982, Colonel Mengistu took personal charge of the 'Red Star' campaign, supposedly the final effort to capture Nacfa and solve the Eritrean problem. It failed, having caused about 30,000 casualties, but it helped to keep the EPLF largely penned up in the north-west, while Mengistu's government tried, with some success, to establish its power in the countryside, particularly around Asmara.

Ethiopian politics in Eritrea

The military solution clearly remained the Ethiopian government's preferred option, but there were various efforts to negotiate a political

A musical band in an Eritrean guerrilla camp. One of the greatest weapons the guerrillas had was their high morale, which groups like this did much to support.

settlement. These did not get far. The Eritreans were suspicious of the government and the Ethiopians believed, understandably, that the EPLF was only interested in independence and would not settle for anything less. A series of ten meetings was held between 1982 and 1985, after the EPLF put forward the idea of a referendum among the Eritrean people to vote on the options for federation, independence or union. No progress was made in the negotiations.

The Ethiopian government did make some efforts to win popular support in Eritrea. In 1978, the army took care to rebuild bridges, roads, houses and shops destroyed in the fighting, and to provide food and shelter for the people.

In 1982, the Red Star campaign was backed up by a development programme which involved a number of government ministries moving to Eritrea for a few months, to organize reconstruction, start new agricultural projects, restore telephone links and provide jobs. Within a few months, however, Mengistu lost interest and the money to finance the projects ran out.

In 1987, the new constitution gave a locally elected assembly in Eritrea control of everything except defence, security and foreign affairs. It was too late. Few Eritreans believed in central government promises, and the EPLF would not accept the government's insistence that any settlement must be within the framework of the existing Ethiopian state.

Politics in Ethiopia

Between 1979 and 1987, the Ethiopian government largely felt it had control of the situation in Eritrea and turned its attention to other problems. A single ruling Marxist party was formed in 1984, the Workers' Party of Ethiopia. Government's attempt to deal with the problems of food shortages and security against guerrilla attacks included large-scale resettlement of famine victims. There was another major

famine in 1984-85, and the government planned to move up to 3 million people from the exhausted lands in the north to fresh lands in the south-west which received more rainfall and had not been over-farmed. Other plans included the creation of co-operative farming, already seen to have failed in Eastern Europe, and villagization.

Villagization brought together groups of small villages into a large one, to make it easier to provide facilities and, of course, to control the population. Either one village was chosen as a centre, or a new village was laid out in a suitable place, with neat rows of houses, a meeting place, and other facilities which included a defending force of troops or armed militia. The villagization policy was greatly resented by people forced to move from their homes into the new centres.

The new villages were seen as security hamlets, and were patrolled by armed militia. In some areas people could go no more than 10 kilometres from the village. 'We are like voiceless prisoners in these places. We have some oxen but not the land to plough. We have the cattle but we can not graze freely. What choice do we have other than to starve?' (Andu Kifle from Inwet.)

The gateway to Harar, the old walled city on the edge of the Ogaden, with pictures of President Brezhnev of the Soviet Union on the left and President Castro of Cuba on the right. It was Soviet arms and Cuban troops that helped to drive back the Somali attack on Harar in 1977.

Mengistu's regime was marked by huge annual Revolutionary Day parades. This one shows the tenth anniversary celebration, when thousands of soldiers, peasants, workers, students and children marched past the leadership in a public display of loyalty and revolutionary 'enthusiasm'. A giant picture of Mengistu is shown presiding over the parade.

Surprisingly, the Eritrean war remained one of the few popular elements in Ethiopian government policy. Most Ethiopians felt that Eritrea was a part of their country and had to be kept. The army continued to support Colonel Mengistu for this reason, although it suffered high losses in the war and was affected by political interference, low pay, bad conditions, constant changes of command and poor morale. Despite all this, and his literally murderous policies, Mengistu received the support that he needed to maintain his position and control during the 1980s because he was so determined to hold on to Eritrea.

He also proved successful in getting military equipment for the war. When this began to fail, as Soviet support was gradually withdrawn after 1987, Mengistu's position was fatally weakened. The Ethiopian government simply did not have the resources to cope with the costs of the war without external help, but had no one to turn to. The USA was appalled by the brutality of Mengistu's regime, and disliked its Marxist ideology. With the collapse of the Soviet Union in the late 1980s, the USA was no longer involved in competition between the superpowers, and had no reason to assist a country formerly in alliance with the Soviets.

GUERRILLAS SEIZE POWER

In the 1980s, the Ethiopian government's position seriously weakened, despite efforts to institutionalize its power. The Workers' Party of Ethiopia, set up in 1984, never inspired enthusiastic support. A draft constitution, approved by referendum in 1987, allowed for five autonomous (mainly self-governing) regions. It proposed giving considerable freedom to Eritrea and Tigrai, as well as to three other regions which, like Tigrai, were ethnically based – one Afar region and two Somali ones. The constitution was at once rejected by the EPLF and the Tigrai People's Liberation Front (TPLF), another opposition movement that had been gaining support since it was formed in 1975.

The economy ran into difficulties as the price of Ethiopia's major export, coffee, tumbled. Imports of cheap Soviet oil stopped in 1989, just as it became apparent that Soviet arms supplies were going to end. The government had made considerable efforts to mobilize agricultural production to prevent famines, but its use of state-run farms was ineffective and expensive. Their failure contributed to the disastrous famine of 1984-85.

The policy of resettlement was brought in on a large scale after 1985. The government moved some 600,000 people from drought-hit areas, particularly in Tigrai and Wollo regions. There were plans to move 3 million in all, not only to relieve the famine areas but to take away support for the guerrillas. In part to try and prevent this, and to obtain international aid on their own account, the TPLF moved 200,000 famine victims into Sudan at the same time. This kept the people away from government food stocks that might tempt them to give their support to the government rather than to the guerrillas.

The resettlement scheme was badly prepared and inadequately supported. Many people were tricked into moving, and given false expectations;

A feeding centre run by the non-governmental agency (NGO), World Vision, operating in a government held area of Ethiopia during the 1984-85 famine. Most international donors insisted on their aid being distributed by NGOs to prevent misuse.

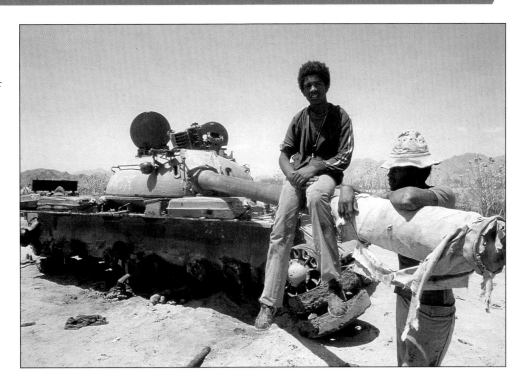

Eritrean guerrillas on a captured Russian-made tank in 1988 at Af Abet, the scene of one of the EPLF's greatest victories. The EPLF captured enough tanks and other armoured vehicles to set up their own tank units before the war ended.

some were driven on to planes and lorries at gunpoint; others were told their food supplies would be stopped unless they went. But a lot did want to move, in the hope of finding something better. The famine was only controlled by an international relief effort that provided grain on an enormous scale.

Another famine threatened in 1989-90, following a highly unpopular villagization programme that seriously reduced food production. None of the government measures helped food supplies but in fact, by the 1980s, food shortages had become more or less permanent. It seems that even in a good year, such as 1991-92, Ethiopia needs to import several hundred thousand tonnes of grain.

The military collapse

In 1988, while the Ethiopian government forces exhausted themselves in a series of attempts to take Nacfa, the EPLF was able to build up its strength. It also provided extensive support for the TPLF. The TPLF, unlike the EPLF, did not want total independence for its region or for the Tigrean people. But it wanted control of Tigrai by Tigreans – in other words, by the TPLF. Like the EPLF, it followed a socialist ideology, but this was based on the stricter example of Chinese communism, rather than the Soviet form.

Relations between the EPLF and the TPLF varied because of their different ideologies, but from 1989, as victory became a real possibility, the two fronts co-ordinated military activity. The TPLF made it clear that it would accept Eritrean independence; in return the EPLF provided troops to assist the opposition movements within Ethiopia.

The first in a series of military disasters for the Ethiopian government came in early 1988. Catching and destroying a convoy in an ambush, the EPLF overran Af Abet, the main headquarters and supply base for the armies facing Nacfa. The government had 15,000 casualties and lost huge amounts of equipment. The next year the TPLF won a series of major victories, again costing the government thousands of casualties. Government troops abandoned Tigrai. The army finally lost patience with Mengistu's refusal to look for a political solution. In May, most senior officers took part in an attempted coup. It failed, and dozens of generals were killed or imprisoned. The army's morale fell further when in February 1990 the EPLF captured the port of Massawa, cutting the army's supply lines in Eritrea.

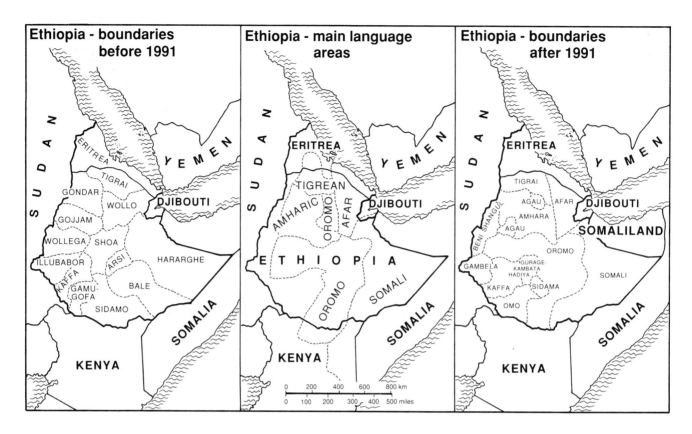

Ethiopia's boundary changes. Ethiopia's regional boundaries under Haile Selassie (above left) were based on historic kingdoms and conquests. The new regions created since 1991 (above right) are based more closely on the languages and cultures of the people; the larger language groups are marked on the central map.

Take-overs in Addis Ababa and Asmara

In Tigrai in 1989, the TPLF set up the Ethiopian People's Revolutionary Democratic Front (EPRDF), incorporating two other organizations that represented the two largest ethnic groups in Ethiopia, the Amharas and the Oromos. It was under the banner of the EPRDF that Addis Ababa was captured in May 1991. President Mengistu had fled to Zimbabwe a week earlier.

At the same time, the EPLF announced that it was setting up its own transitional government in Eritrea. A referendum on Eritrean independence was scheduled for 1993; when finally held, it produced a vote of 99.8 per cent in favour. A two-year delay before the referendum gave time for the EPLF to prove that it could run an efficient and competent administration, and helped to impress the USA, which had preferred that Eritrea remain part of Ethiopia. The EPLF also tried to calm the fears of the African states, many of which felt that they might be threatened by independence movements among minority ethnic groups if these could see the example of a successful movement in Eritrea.

The EPLF committed itself to multi-party democracy in the future, though neither ethnic nor religious parties would be allowed. This

THE ETHIOPIAN PEOPLE'S REVOLUTIONARY
Democratic Front (EPRDF) in 1991 was made up of: Tigrai People's Liberation Front, TPLF (Tigrean); Ethiopian People's Democratic Movement, EPDM (Amhara); Oromo People's Democratic Organization, OPDO (Oromos); Ethiopian Democratic Officers' Revolutionary Movement, EDORM (military). Two other organizations were also associated with it, Beni Shangul People's Liberation Movement, BPLM (the Beni Shangul live in a region of the same name along the Sudan border); Gambella People's Liberation Movement, GPLM (the Nuer people, around the town of Gambella near the Sudan border).

contrasted strongly with Ethiopia, where the EPRDF insisted on ethnic politics. The TPLF had drawn its support from the Tigrean people only. After it dropped its commitment to socialism in the late 1980s and was converted to multi-party democracy, it had little alternative to ethnic politics.

The EPRDF convened a national conference in Addis Ababa in July 1991, setting up a Council of Representatives in which thirty-two, mostly ethnic organizations were represented. Many other parties appeared later. The EPRDF advocated a democratic federal system based on twelve regions and two cities, the capital Addis Ababa and the eastern city of Harar, which was inhabited by a separate nationality, the Adari. The regions were given new boundaries based on ethnicity. Nationalities like the Amhara, which were widely spread, were not favoured by the concentration on separate regions in the new system. The Amhara had been the ruling elite under Haile Selassie and Mengistu, and they identified themselves with strong centralized government.

Local and regional elections were held in Ethiopia in mid-1992, though international observers were critical, referring to abuses of the procedures and much interference in the voting.

The credibility of the new system was weakened by the refusal of the largest Oromo organization, the Oromo Liberation Front (OLF), to take part. The EPRDF's habit of creating its own parties to try and control the regional governments caused considerable resentment. The EPRDF government proved touchy about criticism, despite an apparently genuine commitment to free expression of most political views.

The desire for peace is strong throughout Ethiopia, but the reliance on ethnic politics is also widely seen as a gamble by Ethiopians and outside observers. Critics have argued that government resources will be insufficient to provide for administrations in all twelve regions. Good relations between Ethiopia and Eritrea are necessary for both, particularly because of their geographical relationship. However, ethnic politics pose a long-term threat. The contrast between EPLF and EPRDF policies is striking, as the same Tigrean nationality predominates in both organizations. Tigreans live both in south central Eritrea and in the Tigrai region of Ethiopia; they were divided at the time of Italian colonialism at the end of the last century. It is hard to believe that there will be no pressure for the two areas to come together again at some time in the future.

Eritreans celebrate the independence they fought for 30 years to obtain. Eritrea joined the Organization of African Unity and the United Nations after its formal declaration of independence in May 1993.

SOMALIA FALLS APART

There is a certain parallel in the steady collapse of Mengistu in Ethiopia and of Siad Barre in Somalia. From 1978, there were signs that both governments were in decline. The two presidents were ousted within a few months of each other in 1991. Siad Barre had survived the coup attempt against him in 1978 after the Ogaden defeat, but it left him suspicious of the army. He allowed its unity and professionalism to break down, making promotions and postings on the basis of clan alliances. Siad Barre began to depend only upon his own Marehan clan, on the Ogaden, his mother's clan, and on the Dolbuhunta, the clan of one of his sons-in-law.

A significant part of the problem was the country's shortage of money and resources. In 1980, Somalia only got $93 million for US use of Berbera's air and sea facilities when it changed alliances. The Gulf War of 1980-88 meant Somalis working in the Gulf States sent less money back to Somalia. In 1983, Saudi Arabia banned Somali cattle imports, claiming they were diseased. Cattle were Somalia's major export and a very important source of income. The accusation of disease was quickly proved wrong, but Saudi Arabia never withdrew its ban. Somalis got around it to some extent by exporting cattle to Djibouti and Yemen for onward transport to Saudi Arabia, but this was much less profitable.

Somalia received a lot of international aid for refugees fleeing from Ethiopia in the early 1980s, but by 1985 international agencies were questioning the large numbers of refugees reported by the Somali government. Because of their doubts and because of increasing guerrilla attacks and general insecurity in Somalia, relief agencies and foreign governments became more reluctant to provide aid.

The collapse of the state was emphasized by the position of civil servants, who got no salary increases for many years. When a 10 per cent pay rise was given in 1988 it was estimated that this would provide only one tenth of what was necessary for a family to survive. Civil servants had to take second jobs, accept help from relatives who grew their own food, or accept bribes. In any practical sense, there were no institutions functioning correctly during the 1980s. Government ministers operated their own controls of imports, production and supply. There were no services of the kind normally associated with a state, whether medical, educational or financial, and little law and order.

General Mohammed Siad Barre, President of Somalia 1969-91. Initially a popular figure, his removal in January 1991 was widely welcomed although it set off a bloody and murderous struggle to succeed him.

Skulls from a mass grave near Hargeisa. Relics of Siad Barre's repressive measures are found all over the country – burnt-out tanks, guns and landmines from old battles as well as human bones from massacres and killings.

Guerrilla opposition

Two guerrilla organizations appeared in the early 1980s, the Somali National Movement (SNM) and the Somali Salvation Democratic Front (SSDF). Both claimed to have national support, but the SNM was largely backed by the Isaaq, the main clan of northern Somalia, while the SSDF drew its support from the Majerteen, the major clan of the north-east. Both organizations based themselves across the border in Ethiopia, which allowed Siad Barre to portray them as traitors associating with the Ethiopians, the traditional enemy. However, their location had the advantage for the SNM and SSDF of providing them with support and a secure base.

Siad's main response to guerrilla activities was the creation of militias among clans loyal to him or from whom he could buy support. They were given arms and encouraged to pursue highly destructive tactics against opponents, burning crops and destroying buildings, roads and equipment that might prove useful to the guerrilla forces. The Majerteen were made to suffer after the creation of the SSDF, but the Isaaq were worst affected. In 1988, the SNM nearly captured the main northern town of Hargeisa. Siad Barre used his air force, with planes flown by South African mercenary pilots, to bomb the guerrillas out. Hargeisa was virtually destroyed. Several hundred thousand Isaaq fled across the border into Ethiopia, many being attacked on the way. Government repression did just what the SNM had failed to do; it provided the guerrillas with massive public support in the north and swung almost all of the Isaaq clan behind them.

The end of Siad Barre's regime

The final phase of Siad's rule began in 1986, when he was badly injured in a car crash. While he was out of action, a power struggle began within his own family. His eldest wife, Kadija, a political power in her own right, supported General Maslah, Siad's son, against the claims of Siad's cousin and long-term associate Abdurahman Jama Barre, the foreign minister. Disagreements and manoeuvring continued after Siad's recovery. Both the Marehan and Ogaden clans were split by the disputes. The weakness of the regime was vividly illustrated in January 1990, when Siad dismissed the government to try and bring in opposition figures. A few weeks later he was forced to reinstate the prime minister he had recently sacked as 'a failure'.

SOMALI CLANS

There are six Somali clan families. In order of size these are: Darod (made up of the Dolbuhunta, Majerteen, Marehan, Ogaden and Warsengeli); the Hawiye (mainly divided between the Abgal and the Habr Gidir); the Isaaq (in which the major branches are the Habr Awal, Habr Jaalo, Habr Yunis, Arab and Eidegalla); Rahenwein; Dir (Gadabursi and Issa); and Digil. The clan structure is the basis for Somali politics at all levels, but clan families seldom operate as a unit except against other clan families.

The map shows the areas occupied by the Somali clans and clan families, and the international boundaries that they cross.

More guerrilla movements appeared, most importantly among the Hawiye clan in central Somalia and the main inhabitants of the capital city, Mogadishu, and surrounding areas. The Hawiye's United Somali Congress (USC) had two elements: a guerrilla force headed by General Aydeed operating in the rural areas; and an urban-based, political opposition, largely made up of professional people such as teachers, bankers and civil servants, which produced a series of manifestos calling for change.

In November 1990, Siad Barre armed a small clan in Mogadishu to use against some of the Hawiye in a local city dispute. This escalated into violent conflict. USC guerrillas came into the city; the government used artillery indiscriminately against Hawiye areas and

sparked off a popular uprising. On 27 January 1991, as guerrilla forces closed in on Siad Barre's residence, Villa Somalia, he fled to his home area in the north-west of the country, where he remained for another sixteen months.

Mogadishu was a ruined city, with huge areas devastated by fighting. The Somali state had to all intents and purposes ceased to exist. The army had collapsed, and the administration and bureaucracy were in total disarray. The government's authority outside Mogadishu had disappeared. Power was divided between the various guerrilla leaders and the political parties that had appeared among the clans. But the traditional authority of clan elders had been weakened and they no longer had control over their fighters and the young people of the clans.

SOMALI HISTORY, 1862-1993

1862 France signs treaty getting rights over Djibouti coastal area.

1886 Britain signs treaties with northern Somali clans and declares protectorate.

1889 Italy signs first treaties with southern clans.

1927 Italy establishes full control over southern areas.

1936 Italian Somaliland used as base for Italy's invasion of Ethiopia and take-over of British Somaliland (1940).

1941 Britain takes back British Somaliland and administers Italian Somaliland.

1959 First general election in southern Somalia. Britain agrees independence for the north.

1960 26 June, British Somaliland becomes independent. 1 July, Italian Somaliland becomes independent and the two countries join.

1963-64 War with Ethiopia. Somalia loses.

1969 Army seizes power in Somalia, forming Supreme Revolutionary Council under Major General Mohammed Siad Barre.

1976 Siad Barre reorganizes Somali guerrillas in Ethiopia. Somali Revolutionary Socialist Party set up.

1977 July, Somali army invades Ethiopia. November, Somalia breaks with Soviet Union. Somali army reaches Harar.

1978 Somali army forced to withdraw from Ethiopia. Attempted coup against Siad Barre.

1979-80 Vast movements of refugees into SOmalia as Ethiopian troops re-establish full control in Ogaden. Somali Salvation Democratic Front (SSDF) set up.

1981 Somali National Movement (SNM) set up.

1986 Mengistu and Siad Barre meet in Djibouti to discuss border problems. Siad Barre badly hurt in car crash in May. Rivalry develops among ruling factions while Siad Barre out of action.

1988 Ethiopia and Somalia restore diplomatic relations. Hargeisa bombed in action by Siad Barre's forces against SNM guerrillas.

1989 United Somali Congress (USC) set up as Hawiye opposition movement.

1990 Siad Barre tries to dismiss government. Critical manifestos appear around Mogadishu.

1991 Siad Barre flees from USC guerrillas, who take over Mogadishu and appoint interim President, Ali Mahdi. May, SNM declares northern Somalia independent as Republic of Somaliland. Fighting in Mogadishu between USC factions of Ali Mahdi and General Aydeed.

1992 UN organize ceasefire in Mogadishu. First peace-keeping troops arrive September, US troops arrive December.

1993 US hands back to UN. General Aydeed declared war criminal by UN in June.

Before the fighting began in 1990, Mogadishu was an attractive, largely Italianate port built on the Indian Ocean, dating back a thousand years or so. Between January 1991 and mid-1993 it was virtually destroyed by fighting.

THE UNITED NATIONS AND SOMALIA

The new authorities in Mogadishu after the fall of Siad Barre got off to a very bad start. Immediately after Siad's flight, in early 1991, the USC announced that it had taken over and invited all opposition groups to a national conference. However, two days later the USC appointed an acting president, Ali Mahdi, and installed a new government, mainly consisting of Hawiye clan members who had been involved in the manifesto group. By acting in advance of any conference negotiations, they offended all other clans and angered the Hawiye guerrillas who had fought against Siad Barre. There was immediate and widespread condemnation from the other main organizations: the SNM (Isaaq), the SSDF (Majerteen) and the Somali Popular Movement (Ogaden). The SNM went on to declare the independence of northern Somalia as the Republic of Somaliland in May 1991.

The daily journey to take the bodies out of Mogadishu. The fighting of 1992, to control the areas south and west of the city, prevented distribution of food supplies and led to widespread starvation and thousands of deaths from famine and disease.

Some Somalis objected to the arrival of US forces in Mogadishu in December 1992. Some of the clans resisted the US forces' attempts to disarm them, leading to the US/UNOSOM decision to try to arrest clan leader General Aydeed (see page 35).

In an attempt to bring the various groups together, the President of Djibouti, Hassan Gouled, arranged two conferences in Djibouti city in June and July 1991. The northerners, the SNM, did not attend. A great deal of the discussion at these meetings revolved around a possible division of ministerial posts, and still more over the question of compensation for property destroyed and for deaths in the fighting for Mogadishu. At the same time the Hawiye made it clear that they thought their turn to be in power had come. The other clans did not agree, and the Djibouti conferences produced no reconciliation.

Ali Mahdi's government was faced by splits within the USC and among the Hawiye clan, which has two major divisions – the Abgal sub-clan in and around Mogadishu, and the Habr Gidir in central Somalia. The Abgal (Ali Mahdi's own sub-clan) supported him; the Habr Gidir backed their own guerrilla leader, General Aydeed. The two leaders rapidly developed a personal conflict, which was fuelled by the rivalry between the two sub-clans. The nomadic Habr Gidir despised the 'soft-living' city dwellers and resented what they saw as Ali Mahdi and others stealing the rewards of victory.

> Weapons were cheap and plentiful in Somalia. In 1991, an AK 47 assault rifle cost only $50.00 (ammunition was 12 cents a bullet); a bazooka $200.00; there were even reports that a Russian-made T54 main battle tank could be found for $2000.00 (petrol was provided to drive the tank away, but shells cost extra).

In July 1991, General Aydeed was elected chairman of the USC. Ali Mahdi set up his own USC. Two months later the strains exploded in four days of fighting which left hundreds dead and thousands injured. In November, renewed hostilities broke out and lasted four months. Neither side won. Both sides were exhausted, food supplies were short, ammunition was running out and international bodies refused to supply aid until the fighting stopped. At least 30,000 people had died, tens of thousands more had been injured and hundreds of thousands had fled from the city. Mogadishu was left divided. Aydeed controlled the larger part, with support from the clan occupying the part of the city around the airport. Ali Mahdi had the backing of another Hawiye sub-clan based around the port.

UN intervention

A cease-fire in March 1992 was organized by the UN, but both leaders regarded it as temporary and made efforts to find other clan allies. Ali Mahdi obtained greater support, largely because other clans were worried by General Aydeed's successes following the cease-fire. Aydeed was responsible for defeating an attempt by Siad Barre to return to Mogadishu in April 1992, stopping Siad's Somali National Front forces only 30 kilometres outside the city. Immediately after this victory, General Aydeed chased Siad Barre out of Somalia and into Kenya. Colonel Ahmed Omar Jess, Aydeed's ally, then captured the southern port of Kismayu, though within a few months Kismayu was retaken by supporters of General Morgan, a son-in-law of Siad Barre who was given support by Kenya. General Aydeed's Habr Gidir in central Somalia were also attacked by the SSDF.

This confused but continual fighting led to serious food shortages and crippling famine in certain parts of the country. After publicity in mid-1992, international food aid began to pour in. Distribution was held up by fighting, by the lack of discipline in the various armies, which looted food, and by the need to pay gunmen for protection of the food supplies. After May, the UN began to play a more active role, but there were disputes over control and size of a UN peace-keeping force. At the end of October, the UN Special Representative in Somalia, Ambassador Sahnoun, was pressured into resignation by his opponents in the UN. He had made real progress in getting Somali clan elders to talk to each other, but had been too critical publicly of the work of some UN agencies.

> The need for disarmament of the gunmen was shown by a 13-year-old's comment: 'Many are hardly older than me. The gunmen seem powerful and scare everyone because of the gun. If they do not have the gun, they would be nothing. That's why they must lose their gun. Of course many have become used to violence. So they will probably go and get a knife. But they can only injure one person at a time with a knife...'
> (Quoted in *Somalia, Operation Restore Hope - a preliminary assessment*, Africa Rights, 1993).

Young troops of General Aydeed's Somali Liberation Army of the USC in their 'technical'. The 'technical', a land rover, jeep or small lorry with the top removed and a heavy machine gun or rocket-launcher on the back, has been a favourite weapon in the fighting in Mogadishu.

The US arrival

As the UN appeared to become ineffective, the USA decided to take drastic action to deal with the humanitarian crisis in Somalia. President Bush announced that US troops would be sent in to safeguard food supplies and ensure their distribution to the starving. As 1992 was presidential election year in the USA, the move was variously seen as a grand humanitarian gesture to end the Bush presidency, or as a public relations exercise to ensure that the presidency ended on an upbeat note. The public relations factor was given some credibility by the careful media arrangements to film US marines as they landed in the middle of the night on Mogadishu beaches. They were met by the assembled US press corps, ready to film the landing for live coverage on US prime-time television. It was technically a multi-national force, but the USA provided most of the 30,000 troops sent in.

By April 1993, the USA had achieved a considerable part of its claimed objectives. Food deliveries had been protected and delivery of food to some of the worst-affected areas had been carried out. The US forces had gone some way towards disarming the various Somali 'warlords', but continued lawlessness through the first half of 1993 made it clear there were plenty of weapons left. The US presence also provided the pressure which persuaded fourteen factions to attend a conference in Addis Ababa in March 1993, where they agreed to set up a Transitional National Council to appoint officials and a judiciary, and to organize elected regional councils and a disarmament committee.

These apparent successes set the scene for the UN to take over again in May 1993, though US troops remained as part of the UN forces. The UN representative, Admiral Howe, said UN aims were 'to create a police force, facilitate justice and restore civil processes'. UNOSOM, the United Nations Mission to Somalia, was given the task of setting up an administrative structure to run the country until the Addis agreement was implemented. The UN's mandate was to run for two years, and it was hoped that

GENERAL AYDEED AND UNOSOM

In June 1993, General Aydeed was blamed for the death of 23 Pakistani UN peace-keeping troops in Mogadishu. The US and UNOSOM authorities in Somalia declared their intent to capture him, and brought in élite US Rangers to do so. Embarrassing failures, including the death of 18 US soldiers in a search operation in October, led to a change in US policy. The Rangers were withdrawn and military missions to capture Aydeed came to a halt.

General Aydeed (left) seen here with UN Ambassador Sahnoun, in October 1992.

UNOSOM's job would be finished by May 1995, the date agreed for the mandate to end.

Somaliland, the breakaway republic in the north, remained outside the process. As it struggled to set up an effective administration, it managed to prevent its clan disagreements from degenerating into the confusion seen in the south of Somalia. It largely succeeded, but Somaliland's total lack of resources and the failure of any richer country to provide aid on the scale required meant it could not establish stability. For the first four months of 1993 the clan elders of Somaliland held a conference to agree the future of their state, in the process removing the country's president and replacing him with another. It was an impressive demonstration of what Somali traditional leaders could do without outside interference.

DJIBOUTI

The other country that has been closely involved in the continual conflicts between Ethiopia and Somalia and in the Eritrean struggle is Djibouti, a tiny state which borders all three. Its two main ethnic groups, the Afars and the Issas straddle the borders. Issas, who are Somalis, live in Ethiopia and the northern part of Somalia, or Somaliland. The Afars inhabit the whole of south-eastern Eritrea as well as parts of eastern Ethiopia.

Djibouti has minimal resources and a tiny population – officially just under 500,000 people, of whom about half live in the capital city and port, also called Djibouti. Originally French Somaliland, and then the French Territory of the Afars and Issas, Djibouti became an independent state in 1977. Both Somalia and Ethiopia have always been anxious about the other's influence there.

Djibouti has only two assets. One is its position at the foot of the Red Sea, where the sea narrows and it is easy to control the Bab el Mandeb Straits and prevent ships passing through. This is why the French still keep a military presence there, a garrison of 4,000 troops together with naval and air facilities. It is also a French 'listening post' able to listen to radio and telephone links

Djibouti port, already the largest port in the Horn of Africa and still expanding. It has been historically of great importance to Ethiopia, which is an inland country with no coastline of its own.

The Djibouti-Addis Ababa railway, started in 1897 and completed in 1917, is 782 km long and forms the main link between the two capital cities. There are plans to improve and modernize it.

throughout the Middle East. Djibouti was the base for French participation in the multinational force deployed in Saudi Arabia against Iraq during the crisis after the invasion of Kuwait in 1990-91, and it provided a centre for rest and recreation for the allied troops fighting against Iraq, who were based in the Gulf.

Djibouti's other main assets are its port and the railway which links the port to Addis Ababa, the capital of Ethiopia. The port of Djibouti was established as a free port in 1981 allowing goods to be held or processed there before re-export without customs charges. It now has a deep water container terminal, special loading and unloading facilities, refrigerated warehouses and other improvements. An oil refinery is being constructed and the Djibouti government hopes

that the port will become a major trans-shipment centre as well as a regional port, to serve Ethiopia, Somalia, Eritrea and a number of other neighbouring countries.

Historically, Djibouti was the major port for Ethiopia, because of the building of the Franco-Ethiopian railway from Djibouti to Addis Ababa, completed in 1917. Without the Eritrean coast-line Ethiopia is landlocked. During the Italian control of Eritrea, the railway was Ethiopia's only real outlet to the sea, though some trade went through Zeila in northern Somalia. However, when guerrillas of the WSLF put the Djibouti-Addis Ababa line out of action during the Ethiopia-Somali war of 1977, the Ethiopian government developed Assab, in southern Eritrea, as Ethiopia's main port. It was through

Assab that Soviet arms and relief food were brought during the 1970s and 1980s.

Now Assab is part of independent Eritrea and its only real function is as a port for Ethiopia. All its road links are to Ethiopia. So the Eritreans have made it a free port for Ethiopian use and, for economic reasons, they would prefer Ethiopia to continue to use it, although this will disappoint the government of Djibouti.

Opposition in Djibouti

On independence in 1977, Hassan Gouled, a senior Issa political figure, became president of Djibouti. He subsequently stood as the sole presidential candidate in elections in 1981 and 1987. He was careful to balance his governments, always having an Afar prime minister and six Afar ministers, working with seven Issa ministers. However, power remained firmly in the hands of the president and, by extension, with the Issa. In the 1970s before independence, a unified political movement supporting independence had attracted both Afars and Issas. After independence, the Afars were prevented from setting up their own party and in 1981 Djibouti became a one-party state.

Political opposition inside Djibouti grew on two levels in the 1980s. Afars felt they were becoming more and more marginalized. There were a number of clashes between Afars and

A legacy of colonialism: there are still over 10,000 French residents in Djibouti and goods are flown in daily from France to French-owned supermarkets. The cattle by the roadside suggest a more traditional way of life, but cattle are one of Djibouti's few exports, although most come from Ethiopia and Somaliland.

government security forces in Afar towns. In November 1991, a new opposition group made up of three armed Afar groups, the Front for the Restoration of Unity and Democracy (FRUD), launched a full scale revolt. Within a few weeks they had overrun the Afar areas of the north and were besieging government troops in the two main northern towns of Obok and Tadjurah. Hassan Gouled appealed to France for assistance, under the terms of military agreements by which France had promised help against external enemies of Djibouti. France refused, claiming that FRUD represented internal opposition. One reason for refusal was the hope that FRUD's rebellion might force Hassan Gouled into moderating his policies and allowing a multi-party system that would satisfy the Afars.

There was also opposition to Hassan Gouled from the Issa, concerned that he intended to make his nephew his successor and thus continue the dominance of his own Mamassen sub-clan. Opposition intensified after the ruling party insisted it would remain the sole legal party, in March 1991. Under pressure from France and the FRUD revolt, a new constitution for a multi-party system was agreed and accepted in September 1992. Elections were held in December 1992. The constitution allowed for four parties, but only two took part. A third party was registered, but withdrew before the voting.

There was considerable surprise when Hassan Gouled's ruling party won all the seats. The new constitution allowed the president to stand for a third term of office, which he could not have done under the previous one. In the presidential election of May 1993, Hassan Gouled won surprisingly easily, getting 60 per cent of the votes. FRUD, which had suffered a series of military defeats earlier in the year and lost most of the towns captured earlier, had called on Afars not to vote. The election result did not satisfy any of Hassan Gouled's critics.

Djibouti's international role
Growing uncertainties within Djibouti contrasted with Hassan Gouled's status in the Horn of Africa. Refugees were a major burden on the fragile economy, but Djibouti encouraged voluntary repatriation programmes and tried to keep on good terms with neighbours. Relations with Ethiopia improved when the two countries took over joint control of the railway from the French-Ethiopian company that had run it.

In 1985 Hassan Gouled took a leading role in the setting up of an Inter-Governmental Authority for Drought and Development (IGADD), based in Djibouti, involving Djibouti, Ethiopia, Somalia, Kenya, Uganda and Sudan. Eritrea was also expected to join. IGADD organized funding for joint projects in the region, and it was seen as a possible way towards the creation of an economic community of the Horn. Its first summit meeting played a considerable role in bringing together the then presidents of Ethiopia and Somalia, paving the way to an agreement between the two countries in 1988, for the first time since the Ogaden war of 1977-78.

Djibouti also tried to bring Somali factions together, at two conferences in Djibouti in 1991. This apparent support for the unity of Somalia did not go down well with the self-proclaimed Republic of Somaliland. In turn, Somaliland contacts with FRUD annoyed the Djibouti government. But Djibouti has not been drawn into the conflicts affecting its neighbours in the Horn of Africa, and generally has a stabilizing influence in the region.

DRUG TRADE IN THE HORN OF AFRICA
Many Djiboutians enjoy qat, a mildly narcotic leaf chewed as a stimulant, usually as a social activity over a drink in the afternoon and early evening. Qat is a major export of Ethiopia to Djibouti and to Somaliland where it is also widely enjoyed. In Somalia, where it is called miraa, it is also very popular and flown in from Kenya. Many of the Somalian clan militia units are paid in miraa. Siad Barre tried to ban the trade in the mid-1980s, but it was so valuable that his police and army units then fought to take control of illegal and underground supply routes.

FAMINE AND REFUGEES

'Dawn, and as the sun breaks through the piercing chill of night on the plain outside Korem, it lights up a biblical famine, now, in the twentieth century. This place, say workers here, is the closest thing to hell on earth. The situation in Ethiopia has gone well beyond the stage at which words like tragedy and disaster have any meaning. It's a situation that is out of the control of the government here, or of the international voluntary agencies. It will be nearly a year before Ethiopians can expect proper rains again. By that time, thousands of people, perhaps even millions of people may have died.' (Michael Buerk, BBC, October 1984, Korem, in Ethiopia.)

That television report, with haunting pictures of the suffering of the starving, played the major role in alerting the world to the disaster of the famine in 1984-85 in Ethiopia. Shown in the UK, Europe and the USA, it was an immensely powerful broadcast, with sound and pictures combining to make images impossible to ignore or to forget. Nobody knows how many died in the famine, although estimates range up to 2 million. The most probable figure is around 500,000.

The 1984-85 famine was merely the worst of several in Ethiopia over a number of years. The worst-hit areas were Tigrai and Wollo, which had been the centre of the equally serious drought and famine of 1972-74. But famine and starvation are rarely just the result of drought, and certainly not in Ethiopia and Somalia. Human policies, of governments or liberation fronts, are as responsible. Ethiopia, like Somalia, suffered from inadequate road systems, critical shortages of transport, and diversion of resources into anti-guerrilla struggles. In the 1980s, Ethiopia was the poorest country in the world. Yet between 1977 and 1987 it acquired weapons worth about 8 billion dollars from the Soviet Union (though it is unlikely ever to pay for them).

Famine refugees in Ethiopia in 1985. In the high, cold mountains there was no shelter or fuel, and no food. People poured into the feeding centres and overwhelmed the available supplies.

Distribution of relief aid in Somalia. Aid did finally pour into the famine areas, and the world's response, in Ethiopia in 1984-85 and in Somalia in 1992, was impressive. Equally important was the provision of transport. The quantities of relief goods that needed to be transported were far beyond the government's resources, and hundreds of lorries also had to be donated.

In the wars in Ethiopia in the 1980s, food aid was used as a weapon by all sides. The government tried to tempt people out of guerrilla-held areas by offering food: aid-donated grain fed the troops; relief supplies for guerrilla areas were bombed. Guerrillas attacked vehicles carrying food, and controlled supplies to keep the loyalty of their followers. They took donated grain to feed their fighters and used money provided for grain transport to help fund guerrilla organizations.

The numbers game and food aid

Some policies, whatever the intention, made things worse, notably resettlement in Ethiopia. When 600,000 people were moved, thousands died because of poor organization and preparation. People were transported by bus, truck or plane; some even had to walk to the

> Drought was the original cause for the crop failures in 1984-85. 'For the third year I planted but nothing grew. I sold my ox and continued to live a while longer. But it was useless; there was nothing for me there. I have no future. Even if the rains come again, my ox [for ploughing] is gone and I have no seed to plant. Perhaps I will die here in this camp. Who knows but God?' (Famine victim, Makelle, Ethiopia 1985.)

CHAPTER 10

Food distribution in Korem camp, Ethiopia, in 1984. Good intentions often go wrong: in the early stages of relief aid, all that was available was a handful of roasted grain per person. Without fuel it could not be cooked, and it did more harm than good to young children who could not digest it at all.

resettlement sites. On arrival, they often found difficult conditions, due to lack of money, equipment and trained workers.

But resettlement was merely one of the large-scale population movements affecting the Horn of Africa since the 1970s. Millions fled as refugees from drought, famine and war, as well as through policies like resettlement or villagization. At least 750,000 Eritreans crossed into Sudan, and at least 200,000 other Ethiopians. Over half a million people were displaced inside Ethiopia during the fighting in the south in the 1980s, and as many in the north. Djibouti received about 50,000 refugees after the Ogaden war, and another 90,000 from Somalia after 1988. Estimates of refugee flows across the Somali-Ethiopian border included claims of 1.3 million from Ethiopia to Somalia in 1978-80; several

hundred thousand returning in the mid-1980s; and about 400,000 fleeing from northern Somalia into Ethiopia in 1988.

There was often disagreement over the numbers of people in the feeding camps and refugee centres. In Somali camps in 1987, a figure of 850,000 was agreed for planning purposes, but claims ranged from the government's 1.3 million to the 400,000 estimated by one agency. Where checks were made, figures were always found to be exaggerated. In 1987, a large number of people fleeing from villagization in Ethiopia arrived in one camp. Records of arrivals showed that after several months there were 90,000 in the camp, but the amount of water used suggested a much smaller number. When a head count was made, it turned out there were only 32,000 people in the camp.

Disease - the real killer

The tragedy of the Horn of Africa lies with ordinary people caught up in years of war and famine, and suffering their effects. Starvation is not usually the major killer, even during a disastrous famine. It is more likely to be epidemic diseases, caused by the concentration of vast numbers of people in feeding centres and by poor hygiene. In Ethiopia in 1972-74, when the government ignored the crisis and did not set up shelters, many did die of starvation. But in Somalia at the same time, where people were put into relief shelters, the deaths came from dysentery, pneumonia, malaria and tuberculosis. In the camps in Somalia after 1978, the great killers were measles and diarrhoea. The same thing happened in Ethiopia in 1984-85, and in Somalia in 1992. Malnutrition, of course, contributes to the ease with which people, particularly children, are affected by disease.

The politics of food aid

Major international agencies do an excellent and vital job in relieving famines, but they do sometimes forget who they are helping and why. The US-UN and international agency relief operation in Somalia came under a lot of criticism in 1992 and early 1993 for failing to employ qualified Somali professionals on any large scale, preferring to use their own experts. When they become caught up in local conflicts, there is a real danger that the agencies can be diverted from their original purpose. In the 1980s, aid to Ethiopia played a major role in prolonging the conflicts. Aid-donated food relief helped to support the government of Mengistu Haile Mariam in 1984-85. But international agency food supplies to the guerrilla factions, the EPLF and TPLF, ensured their survival and eventual victory.

Since the 1970s, ideologies such as communism, Marxism and nationalism in Ethiopia, Eritrea and Somalia have produced leaders prepared to fight to the death with their people's lives. It is impossible to isolate blame, all are guilty to a greater or lesser extent. The effects of the turmoil on the ordinary people of the Horn of Africa are reflected in these words from an Eritrean peasant in 1986: 'We do not know who is our friend, who is our enemy. All we know is that we cannot go back to the place where we were born.'

The Live Aid concert in London, in 1985, when ten hours of rock music in Britain and the USA raised $100 million for Bob Geldof's Live Aid appeal. It was a most moving and impressive people's response to the famine, and did much to shame governments into greater reaction.

CHAPTER 11

PROSPECTS FOR THE FUTURE

In 1993 there was more optimism in all the countries of the Horn. Most of the guns had fallen silent in Ethiopia. There had been two years of good rain and record harvests. A successful conference of Somali leaders in Addis Ababa in January suggested the possibility of reconciliation. A real international effort was being made to restore Somalia as a state. The north, as the Republic of Somaliland, had managed to keep out of the confusion and troubles that afflicted the south, although its independence was still unrecognized. A new state appeared in May 1993 when Eritrea became independent and was accepted into the United Nations.

Yet enormous problems remained. Ethiopia was involved in a bold political experiment with great potential dangers. The regimes in Ethiopia and in Eritrea have inherited a legacy of tens of thousands of people wounded, crippled, orphaned or traumatized by war and famine. The social effects will be apparent for many years in both countries, and in Somalia too. Generations have been brought up to kill and to fight. There are literally millions of weapons in these countries, and hundreds of thousands of people trained to use them.

HUMAN RIGHTS

Human rights have not had much respect in the Horn of Africa for at least 20 years. Tens of thousands of people were killed in both Somalia and Ethiopia under the regimes of President Siad Barre and President Mengistu Haile Mariam. Torture and imprisonment without trial were common. Towns and villages were bombed, and terror was used as a policy to try and break the strength of the opposition.

Since 1991, human rights violations have continued, but on a much smaller scale. In Ethiopia, the international human rights organization, Amnesty International, has catalogued thousands of people detained without trial, including women and children, reports of torture and ill-treatment and deliberate killings. Opposition groups have also been accused of killings and other abuses. In Somalia, the inter-clan fighting of 1991-92 led to widespread killing, torture and mutilation of civilians.

Old habits die hard, and none of the organizations in power have any habit of democracy. Democracy is difficult to acquire for organizations that have, for twenty or so years, operated in a highly centralized, autocratic and secretive fashion as the TPLF and EPLF have done. In Ethiopia, the EPRDF government plans to form an ethnically based federal system, but is likely to control it by creating parties from its own supporters in each ethnic group. There have already been indications that traditional rivalries may re-emerge. In Eritrea, the EPLF stated that multi-party elections would be unlikely before 1997, and limited its democracy in advance to ensure that ex-members of the ELF do not try to build up opposition to the government. Delaying the election was intended to allow the EPLF time to organize the country's political future effectively.

In 1993, Somalia's future appeared to rest in the hands of UNOSOM, the UN body given authority over Somalia to provide food relief, restore civil society and bring anarchy to an end, ultimately allowing the Somali people to choose a new government peacefully and democratically. The fighting in Somalia has devastated large areas of the south; the cost of restoring a functioning government will be immense. In mid-1993, UNOSOM was being criticized for putting ten times as much funding into military operations as into humanitarian affairs. For Somalia to recover, this ratio would need to be reversed before UNOSOM's departure in 1995.

The plans, realistic or otherwise, for Ethiopia, Eritrea, Djibouti, Somalia and Somaliland, all have one thing in common. They need funding, which will be increasingly hard to find. None of these countries have significant resources. Aid from other countries is being attached to tough conditions on human rights. These are to be welcomed, but make it harder for the governments of the Horn to get help. Human rights have certainly improved, but there are still many concerns about the situation.

Peace will encourage greater agricultural production, but Ethiopia does appear to have a permanent and growing shortage of food. Better drought-warning systems, with long-term development aid may help. The danger of famine remains, however, while resources are so small. Eritrea is in an even worse position. The years of fighting have left it devastated, with a huge repair job necessary on roads, bridges and other facilities. In 1992, about 70 per cent of the population relied on food aid, and this will continue for some time.

Both Eritrea and Ethiopia are aware of the need for close relations. Their leaders have not ruled out the possibility of a confederation of the two independent states. It would make good economic sense, as it would to incorporate Djibouti and Somalia, whether as one or two states. Democracy, federation of the new regions in Ethiopia and an economic community for the region – all offer ways forward. They need funding, goodwill, and statesmanship, all of which are still in very short supply.

In Somalia's civil wars, guns meant availability of food. With a written language only twenty years old, education carried on despite ruined schools and no books, chairs, desks, paper or pencils. Food is coming, education is restarting. Both need huge resources before normal life can be fully restored.

GLOSSARY

Afars Nomadic pastoral people living in southern Eritrea, eastern Ethiopia and northern Djibouti.

AK 47 The Kalashnikov AK 47 rifle has been the main weapon of both guerrillas and armed forces in the Horn of Africa. Made in Russia and Eastern Europe, it is a most effective weapon, widely and cheaply available.

Amharas One of the two largest nationalities in Ethiopia, which provided the ruling elite until 1991. The Amharas are Christian agriculturalists living in the central highlands of Ethiopia.

Amnesty International An organization devoted to trying to improve the state of human rights throughout the world by non-violent means.

Autocrat A ruler with absolute power, or someone who behaves as if they have such power.

Bureaucracy A name given to government administrations staffed by civil servants. This word is often used to suggest a slow and incompetent administration with too many staff and too many unchangeable rules.

Clan A division of society – in Somalia clans form the basis for all political allegiances. Somali clan families are divided into clans and sub-clans, and will act together according to the level of opposition that they face.

Confederation The joining together of independent states in some form of loose union. It implies equality of those involved, not a central authority as in a federation (see below).

Darod The largest of the Somali clan families. Its three most important components are the Marehan, the Majerteen and the Ogaden. The Darod live in both north and south Somalia and in Ethiopia.

Derg Amharic for committee, and the name given to the group of just over 100 soldiers who took power in Ethiopia in July 1974.

ELF (Eritrean Liberation Front) The original anti-Ethiopian guerrilla movement in Eritrea. Set up in 1958, it started armed struggle in September 1961. Largely Muslim-supported, it was defeated by the EPLF in civil war in 1981-82 and driven out of Eritrea, when it split into factions.

EPLF (Eritrean People's Liberation Front) A guerrilla organization set up in Eritrea in the early 1970s, originally formed from an alliance of three groups that broke away from the ELF in 1969. Largely designed to appeal to Christians as well as Muslims, it proved the most efficient Eritrean organization in the struggle for independence and took power in Eritrea in 1991.

EPRDF (Ethiopian People's Revolutionary Democratic Front) The organization set up by the TPLF in 1989, incorporating movements for Amharas and Oromos. It is widely seen as Tigrean-controlled. The EPRDF took power in Addis Ababa in May 1991.

Ethnicity Belonging to a particular ethnic group which has its own particular characteristics, of language, nationality, history, culture or religion.

Federation A system of government in which different political (or ethnic) groups have certain powers of self government, but also recognize the authority of a central administration. Nigeria and the USA have federal governments. See also confederation.

Hawiye The largest single southern clan family and one of the three main divisions of the Somali people, the others being the Isaaq and the Darod.

Ideology A set of ideas and beliefs which forms the basis of a political or economic theory or system of government.

Isaaq The main northern clan family in Somalia, and the largest clan in Somaliland. See also SNM.

League of Nations The international body set up after the First World War to try and maintain peace between nations. It was replaced in 1948 by the United Nations.

Militia An armed organization, official or unofficial, but not part of the armed forces.

Multinational Composed of people originating from different nations.

Ogaden The area of south-eastern Ethiopia largely inhabited by Somalis of the Ogaden clan, one of the members of the Darod clan family.

Oromos One of the two largest nationalities in Ethiopia, living across much of the west, south and east of the country. Many Oromo areas were incorporated into the Ethiopian empire at the end of the nineteenth century. The most significant Oromo political movement is the Oromo Liberation Front.

Protectorate A territory or state controlled and protected by a stronger state.

Red Terror The name given to the government repression in Ethiopia carried out against its opponents in 1977-78. The Red Terror was contrasted with the 'White Terror' of the opposition. The names come from the period at the beginning of the Russian Revolution (1917-18), when communists were called Reds and Tsarists were called White Russians.

Resettlement An Ethiopian government social project, which involved resettling famine victims from infertile lands to more productive farming areas. It also had the effect of weakening opposition support.

Self-determination The concept that a people have the right to choose their own future. Much used by nationalities within Ethiopia to justify their opposition to the central government.

SNM (Somali National Movement) The anti-Siad Barre organization set up in 1981. It attempted to be a national movement, but was never more than a northern (Isaaq) movement in reality. Launched large-scale guerrilla operations in 1988 in northern Somalia and took power there after Siad's fall, in the self-proclaimed Republic of Somaliland.

SSDF (Somali Salvation Democratic Front) An anti-Siad Barre organization created in 1979. Essentially a Majerteen movement, though, like the SNM, it claimed to be national. After 1991, it set up its own administration in the north-east (Majerteen areas) of Somalia.

Tigrai The region of Tigrai lies south of Eritrea, and is now the northern region of Ethiopia. It is the home of the Tigrean people (who also live in southern Eritrea).

TPLF (Tigrai People's Liberation Front) A guerrilla organization founded by a group of twenty ex-students in Tigrai, in 1975, to fight for self-determination. It is the major element within the EPRDF.

UN (United Nations) The United Nations is the international body formed in 1945 (at the end of the Second World War) with the principal aim of keeping world peace. All states have a right to membership and to participate in the General assembly. The UN Security Council numbers fifteen countries of which five are permanent council members – Britain, China, France, the Soviet Union and the USA.

USC (United Somali Congress) The political organization of the Hawiye. Set up in 1989 and promptly divided, it also produced two guerrilla organizations, one led by General Aydeed, of the Habr Gidir sub-clan,

and the other by Ali Mahdi, of the Abgal.

Villagization A policy of bringing people from outlying villages and farms into a centralized village where facilities could be provided cheaply, and political control could be exercised more easily. It was widely carried out in Ethiopia in 1985-89 as a security measure.

WSLF (Western Somali Liberation Front) Originally a guerrilla movement against Haile Selassie in the Ogaden region of Ethiopia, it was reorganized by Siad Barre in 1976 as part of his preparations for the invasion of Ethiopia in 1977. Somalia fought the war in the name of the WSLF.

FURTHER INFORMATION

Newspapers and reference
Serious newspapers cover the Horn of Africa to a limited extent when there are crises, but not otherwise. Larger reference libraries have *Keesing's Record of World Events*. *Africa Contemporary Record*, published monthly, covers the area in detail, as does *Africa Confidential*, a fortnightly newsletter, though both cover all of Africa. *Africa, South of the Sahara*, published annually by Europa, provides detailed information on all the countries.

General reading
Bairu Zewde *A History of Ethiopia 1955-1974* (1991)
Hama Tuma *Of Spades and Ethiopians* (poems published by the Free Ethiopia Press, P.O. Box 57069, Washington DC, 1991)
Kaplan, Robert D. *Surrender or Starve: the wars behind the famine* (Boulder, 1988)
Lewis, I. M. *The Modern History of Somalia: Nation and State in the Horn of Africa* (Westview Press, 1988)
Loughram, A.S., et al (eds) *Somalia in word and image* (1986)
Makinda, Samuel M. *Superpower Diplomacy in the Horn of Africa* (Croom Helm, 1987)

More advanced books
Africa Watch Report *Evil Days - 30 Years of War and Famine in Ethiopia* (Human Rights Watch, 1991)
Adnagatchew Tiruneh *The Ethiopian Revolution 1974-87* (Cambridge University Press, 1993)
Clapham, D. *Transformation and Continuity in Revolutionary Ethiopia* (Cambridge University Press, 1986)
Clarke J. *Ethiopia's Campaign against Famine* (Harney & Jones, 1987)
Dawit Wolde Giorghis *Red Tears: War, Famine and Revolution in Ethiopia* (Red Sea Press, 1989)
Erlich, H. *The Struggle over Eritrea 1962-78* (Hoover Institute, 1983)
Hammond, J. *Sweeter than Honey: Testimonies of Tigrean Women* (Links Publications 1989)
Korn, D. A. *Ethiopia, the United States and the Soviet Union* (Croom Helm, 1986)
Markakis, J. *National and Class Conflict in the Horn of Africa* (Zed Books, 1990)
Niggli, P. *The Spoils of Famine: Ethiopian Famine Policy and Peasant Agriculture* (Cambridge, Mass, 1988)

Novels
The Ethiopian and Somali revolutions have not produced a great deal of literature in English, though the Somali novelist Nuruddin Farah, who writes in English, has written a series of books about Somalia under Siad Barre. Among his novels are *From A Crooked Rib* (Heinemann 1970), *A Naked Needle* (Heinemann 1976) and *Maps* (Pan 1986), and an anti-government trilogy which is highly political, *Sweet and Sour Milk* (1980), *Sardines* (1982) and *Close Sesame* (1983).

Ethiopia has a very rich tradition of writing in Amharic but much less has been published in English. Works include *Shinegar's Village* by Sahle Selassie and *The Thirteenth Sun* by Daniachew Worku (both Heinemann, 1973). Writers like Baalu Girma and Hadis Alamayahu have written in Amharic only. Baalu Girma was one of the victims of the revolution, killed because of disapproval of his novel *Oromay* (Kuraz Publishing Agency, 1983). Several foreigners have also written fictional accounts of Ethiopia including Thomas Keneally's, *Towards Asmara* (published, 1989), openly supportive to the EPLF.

Poetry
Poetry has a particularly important role in Somalia's society and is used for political debate as well as more personal subjects. Most Somali poetry has not been translated, but an introduction can be found in Andrzejewski, B W., and Lewis, I.M. *Somali Poetry: An Introduction* (Oxford University Press, 1964), in which thirty-one Somali poems are translated.

Films
Neither Ethiopia nor Somalia have been much used for film-making, largely because of conflict. Neither country has much in the way of a film industry. There have been many television documentaries about events there, but these are mainly concerned with famine and the famine relief camps. Guerrilla fronts have produced their own material, including *Scorched Earth*, a TPLF film of Ethiopian government atrocities (available from Third World First, 232 Cowley Road, Oxford); *The Forbidden Land* (Alter Cine Inc., Daniele LaCourse and Yuan Patry, September 1989); and *A Fight to the Death*, (Alter Cine Inc., Daniele Lacourse and Yuan Patry, April 1990).

INDEX